KING ME!

How many crowns can you find in this picture?

BEACH BATCH

Betty and Boris spent an entire day at the beach building sand castles. When they were done, they noticed that one pair of castles matched exactly. Can you find the matching pair before the tide comes in?

Answer on page 47.

PIPE SCENES

How many differences can you find between these two scenes?

Illustrated by Barbara Gray

SYMPHONY SEARCH

You are the conductor for this silly symphony. Take note and get a good score if you can find these 22 instruments. Look across, backwards, up, down, and diagonally.

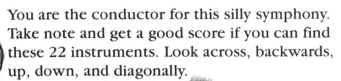

Banjo
Bass
Bassoon
Cello
Clarinet
Drum
Flute
Guitar
Harp
Harpsichord
Horn

Oboe
Organ
Piano
Recorder
Saxophone
Trombone
Trumpet
Tuba
Ukulele
Viola
Violin

```
F L U T E C I O V E S P
B A N J O N A I P B R O
G R C N I L O I V A R L
U K U L E L E B H S E L
I D S N A G R O M S C E
T Z S M U R D A B O O C
A H A R P S I C H O R D
R U B T H O R N L N D T
S A X O P H O N E J E N
A B U T R U M P E T R Y
```

Answer on page 47.

CH CHALLENGE

Check this out. Words beginning with the sound of CH are pictured on these pages. How many can you find? Chalk up more than 30 words and you're a champion.

9

SPEAKING SPANISH

Read the sentences and circle the picture that matches
the Spanish word which is in all uppercase letters.
If your sentences make sense, you will know five new
Spanish words to try on your friends. The way to
pronounce the word is in parentheses after each sentence.

1. The GATO ate a tuna fish sandwich. (Gah-toe)

2. Maria rode a yellow CAMIÓN to school. (Kah-me-yown)

3. A healthy bunny eats a ZANAHORIA every day. (Sah-nah-oar-e-ah)

4. Lopez returned the LIBRO to the library. (Lee-bro)

 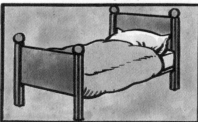 

5. The PERRO dug up his bone. (Peh-rro)

Illustrated by Terry Rogers

Answer on page 47.

DOT MAGIC

What holds many notes but can't play any instruments, and has more letters than the alphabet? To find the answer to this riddle, connect the dots.

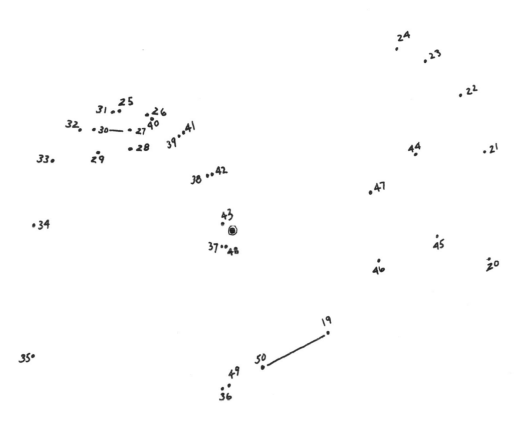

AT THE PARK

The pictures will tell you what to write in the spaces across or down.

Across

Down

Illustrated by Melvin Conrad

STAR SUMS

The empty circles connecting these stars should contain a single-digit number, 1-9, so that the five numbers around each star add up to exactly 30. All the numbers around each star must be different from one another, though some numbers will appear more than once on different stars.

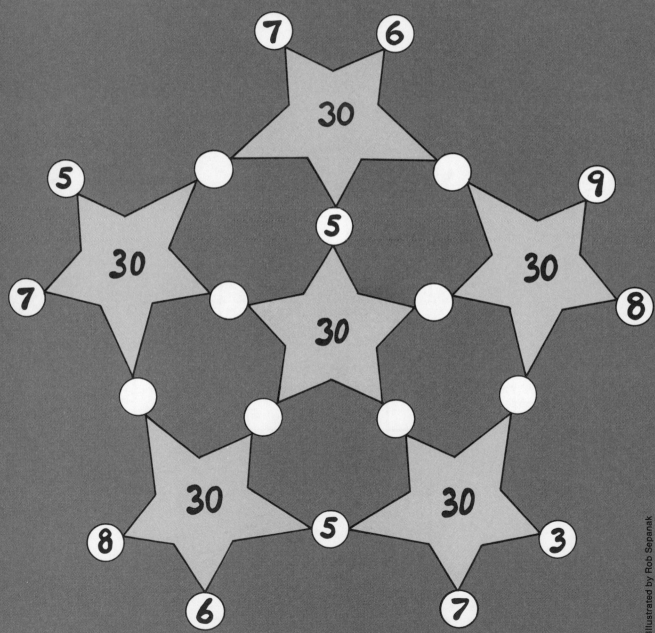

Illustrated by Rob Sepanak

Answer on page 48.

OFF-ROAD MEMORIES

Take a long look at this picture. Try to remember everything you see in it. Then turn the page, and try to answer some questions about it without looking back.

DON'T READ THIS UNTIL YOU HAVE LOOKED AT "Off-Road Memories—Part 1" ON PAGE 15.

OFF-ROAD MEMORIES   Part 2

Can you answer these questions about the off-road scene you saw? Don't peek!

1. Where was this scene taking place?
2. What color were the pennants?
3. Which number car was in the lead?
4. What color was car 29?
5. When was the next race?
6. How many people had hot dogs?
7. Who was working on his motorbike?
8. What was wrong with it?

Answer on page 48.

ON THE SCENT

How can you keep a skunk from smelling?

To learn the answer to this riddle, start with the letter B in the wheel. Go clockwise and copy down every third letter. Continue until you have all 16 letters. Use the blanks below for your answers.

— — —   — — — — — — — —   — — — —   — — — —

Illustrated by Lynn Adams

     Answer on page 48.

WHAT'S IN A WORD?

An automobile can drive almost anywhere in search of new words. More than 40 words of three letters or more, like BOOM or MILE, can be found by using the letters in AUTOMOBILE. Use your drive to see how many of these words you can find.

Answer on page 48.

AUTOMOBILE

Illustrated by John Nez

LOOK OUT BELOW!

Can you answer the crab's question? Follow the directions to find the letters you need. Put each letter in the right spaces, placing the same letters on spaces with similar numbers. When you're done, you will find the answer, as well as the location of the missing baby.

1 2 3 4 5 6 7 8 8 9 10 1

Dive way down below the kelp to find letter number 7.
In the treasure chest lies the third letter.
The ninth letter is hanging from the sea horse's tail.
Explore the sunken wreck. The second letter is in the porthole. The
eighth letter is on the steering wheel.
The clam is holding the fifth letter, while the shark has the tenth letter.
The crab's letter is a phony, but the starfish has the real sixth letter.
The fourth letter is sticking out of the sand.
Watch out for the ray who has a false letter.
You can find letter number one in the ship's crow's nest, along with
the sleeping baby.

Answer on page 48.

Illustrated by Lynn Adams

ONE WRONG WORD

One word in each of these sentences makes the statement wrong. Your job is to find that word and to tell what's wrong about it.

1. Lincoln became president because many men and women voted for him.
2. The ground in the pine forest was covered with big brown leaves in the fall.
3. Aunt Cassie just bought a bigger cage for her pet passenger pigeon.
4. Mr. Frank planted carrots in his garden so that his family could have them in ten days.
5. The glider pilot got more gas for the next flight.
6. When the electricity was off during the lightning storm, the Brown's quartz kitchen clock stopped.
7. In 1930, the city council named a street after a famous astronaut.
8. The diamond cutter used a steel file to shape a new diamond.
9. Ms. Clark has new contact lenses with gold frames.
10. Uncle Matt wrote a nonfiction book about things he made up.

Answer on page 48.

Illustrated by Paul Richer

INSTANT PICTURE

What goes up when rain comes down?
To find out, fill in every section that contains two dots.

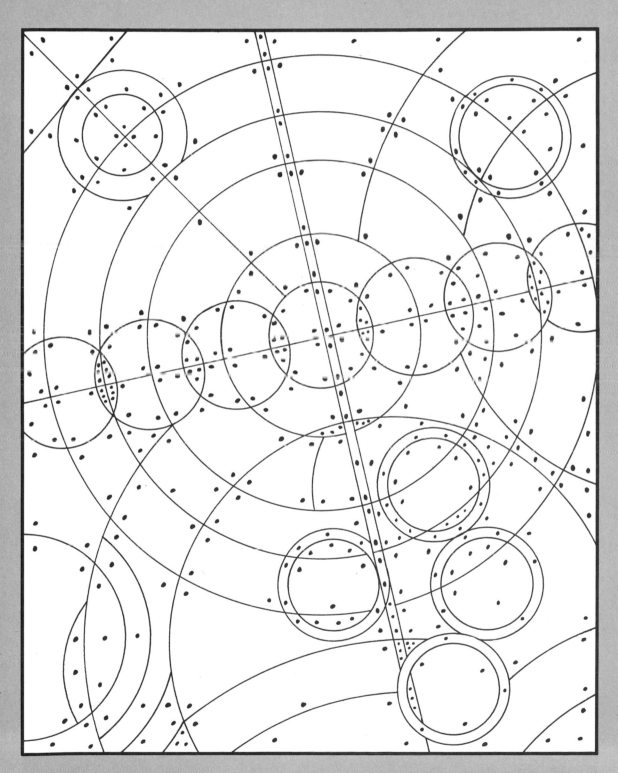

Illustrated by Rob Sepanak

Answer on page 48.

COMBO-CONNECTION

The Puzzleton safe has a very difficult combination. See if you can crack it open by putting all the combinations below in the right boxes. The bank manager left the first set in to get you started. It may help to cross each combination off the list once you find where it belongs.

3 Numbers

106	211	340	518	902
107	213	434	692	967
108	308	502	765	

4 Numbers

0842	1464	4362	6193	9097
1024	1865	5318	7218	9846
1224	1955	6151	7474	
1266	2137	6187	8722	

5 Numbers

02076	31809	51113	85143
08594	33695	51239	86555
13358	40521	51368	
20713	40639	51611	
20714	48765	74325	

6 Numbers

105247	~~487693~~	572091
251394	508319	762195
359182	561502	897012

FIRST NATIONAL BANK

OF

PUZZLETON

487693

Answer on page 48.

BRAID TEASER

Sally, Cindy, Samantha, and Stacy are having a slumber party. During the pillow fight, their braids all got tangled together. Can you figure out which braids belong to which girl?

Illustrated by Melvin Conrad

Answer on page 48.

A FEW GOOD MEN

Twelve different MEN appear in the words below. Use the clues to help fill in the rest of the letters for them.

1. The end of a prayer: __ m e n

2. A very short period of time: __ __ m e n __

3. Having to do with the mind: m e n __ __ __

4. Glue or concrete: __ __ m e n __

5. A wise and trusted teacher: m e n __ __ __

6. A problem or threat: m e n

7. Huge, enormous: __ __ m e n __ __

8. The stomach: __ __ __ __ m e n

9. To start or begin: __ __ __ m e n __ __

10. Sidewalk or driveway: __ __ __ __ m e n __

11. The wire inside a lightbulb: __ __ __ __ m e n __

12. A collection of animals: m e n __ __ __ __ __

Answer on page 49.

25

PICTURE MIXER

Copy these mixed-up squares in the spaces on the next page to put this picture back together. The letters and numbers tell you where each square belongs. The first one, A-3, has been done for you.

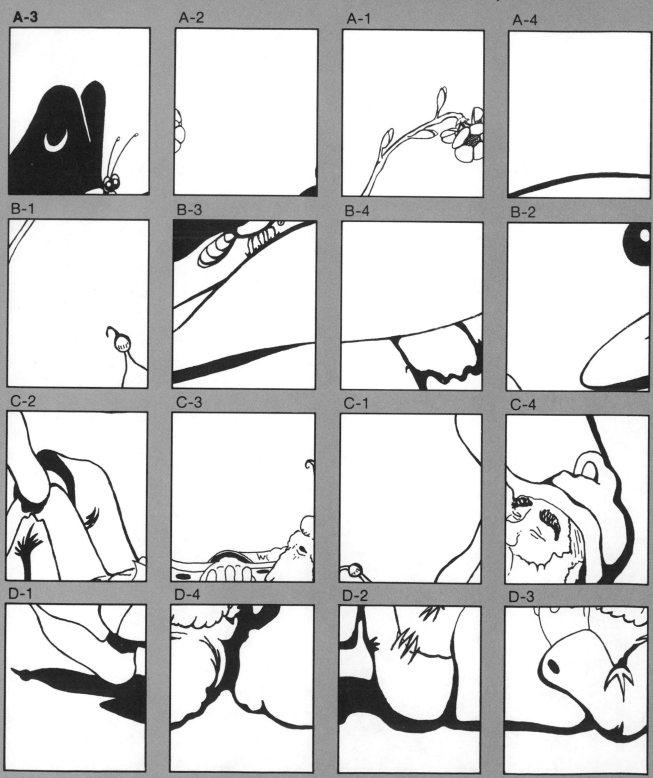

A-3 A-2 A-1 A-4

B-1 B-3 B-4 B-2

C-2 C-3 C-1 C-4

D-1 D-4 D-2 D-3

A

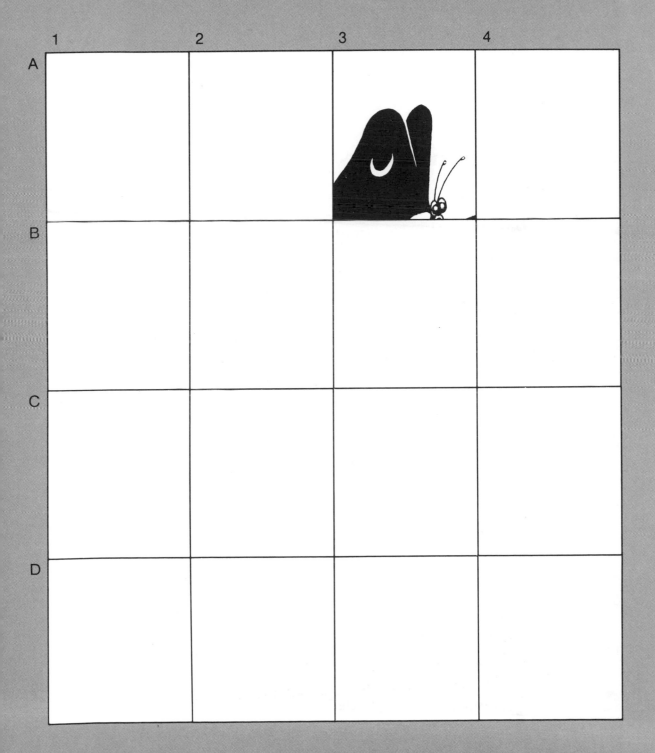

B

C

D

Answer on page 49.

PARTY PROBLEMS

Penelope is planning a party. But the printer proved to be a problem.

Each word in the invitation below was printed in alphabetical order so that most of the words are scrambled. Can you help Penelope unscramble the letters so the party can proceed?

aeelPs cemo ot my abdhirty aprty hist addeensWy aefrt isx c'ckloo. eW illw aehv acek, cei acemr, adn ados opp. eW illw acden, alpy aegms, adn gins gnoss. It illw be lost fo fnu. eHop ouy acn cemo!

eLov,
eeelnopP

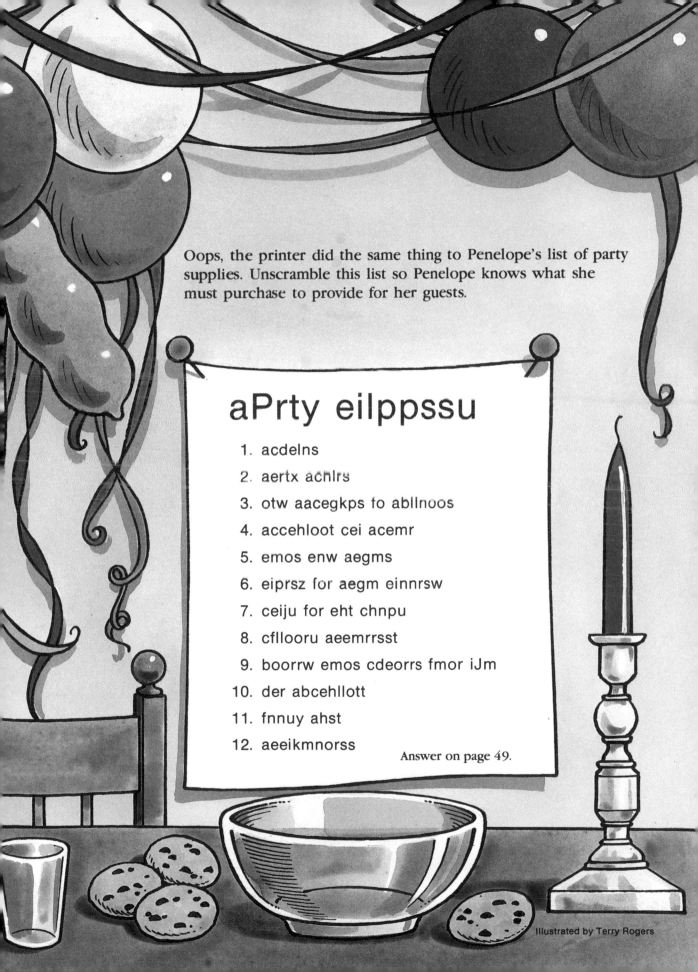

Oops, the printer did the same thing to Penelope's list of party supplies. Unscramble this list so Penelope knows what she must purchase to provide for her guests.

aPrty eilppssu

1. acdelns
2. aertx achlrs
3. otw aacegkps fo abllnoos
4. accehloot cei acemr
5. emos enw aegms
6. eiprsz for aegm einnrsw
7. ceiju for eht chnpu
8. cfllooru aeemrrsst
9. boorrw emos cdeorrs fmor iJm
10. der abcehllott
11. fnnuy ahst
12. aeeikmnorss

Answer on page 49.

Illustrated by Terry Rogers

SIZE WISE

Though they look it here, all these objects are not the same size. Put a number in each box, so that they will all be listed in the order of their size, from smallest to largest. The first one has been numbered to get you started.

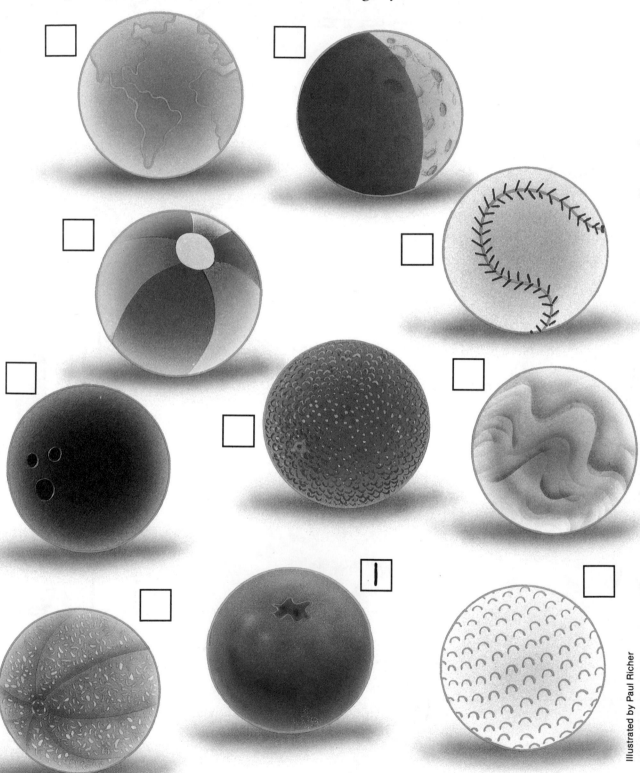

Illustrated by Paul Richer

Answer on page 49.

STOP, LOOK, AND LIST

Under every category, list one thing that begins with each letter. For example, one place to meet people that begins with "C" is a Concert. See if you can name another.

Places to Meet People

C _____

A _____

G _____

M _____

T _____

Insects

C _____

A _____

G _____

M _____

T _____

Metals

C _____

A _____

G _____

M _____

T _____

Illustrated by Lisa Dayer

Answer on page 49.

GEOLOGY GEMS

A geologist is a scientist who studies rocks, stones, minerals, and gems. See if you can mine the code below to pick out the elements that will solve the geological jokes on the next page.

Illustrated by John Nez

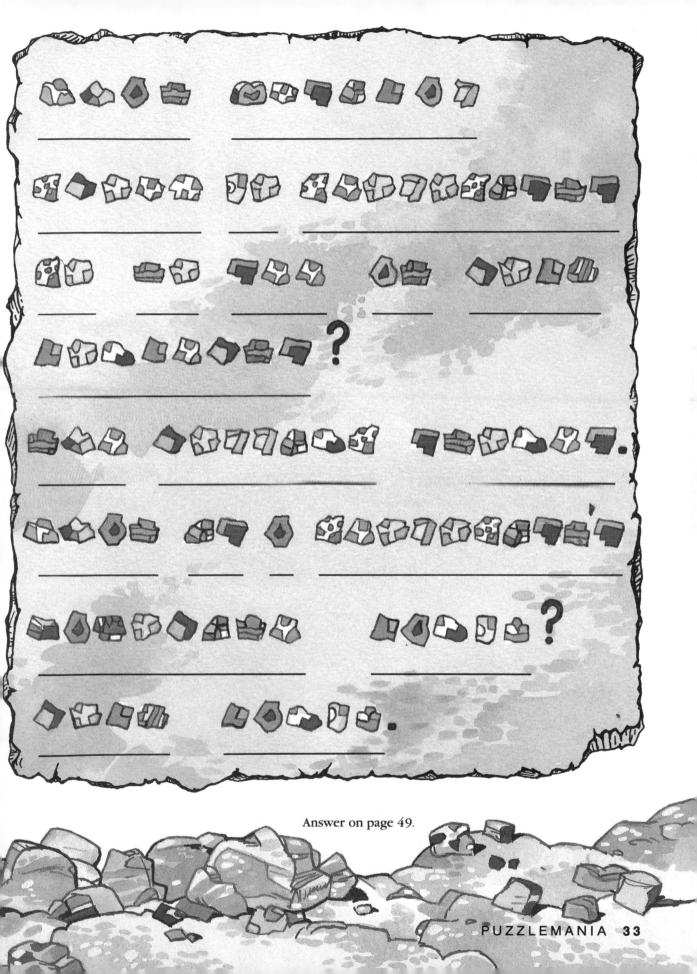

Answer on page 49.

RAINBOW ROUND-UP

What color would you paint each group of things?

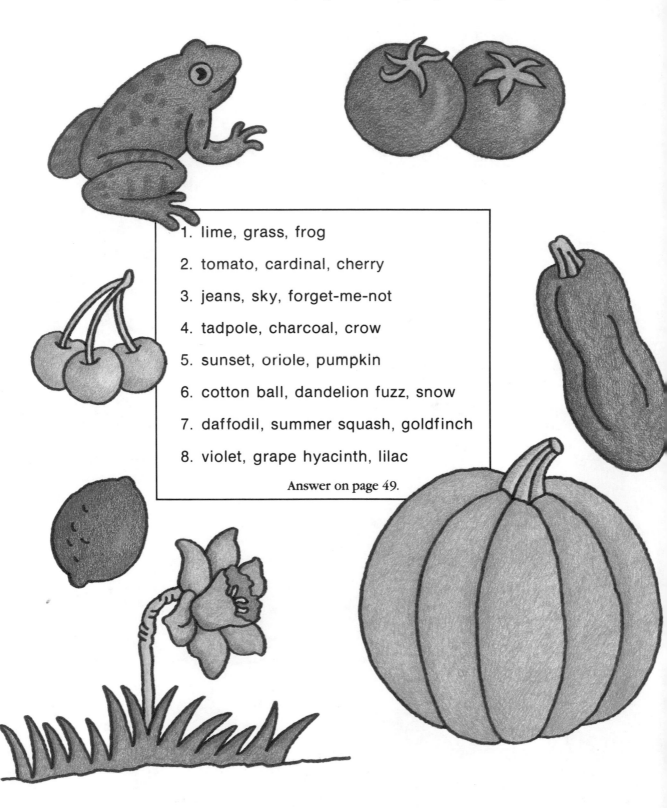

1. lime, grass, frog

2. tomato, cardinal, cherry

3. jeans, sky, forget-me-not

4. tadpole, charcoal, crow

5. sunset, oriole, pumpkin

6. cotton ball, dandelion fuzz, snow

7. daffodil, summer squash, goldfinch

8. violet, grape hyacinth, lilac

Answer on page 49.

Illustrated by Barbara Gray

VEGETABLE SOUP

A garden of vegetables is hidden in the sentences below. These vegetables are growing in two or more words with the letters in sequence and not jumbled. How many can you pick out?

For example: Eric or Neil will bring the food. The vegetable CORN is hidden in the words "EriC OR Neil."

1. Johnny wants to be an astronaut someday.
2. Karyn used the recipe again because it was so good.
3. Jim took rabbit pellets out to the animals.
4. The museum curator said the urn must be Etruscan.
5. Why am I having so much trouble with spelling?
6. Won't Rifka let you in?
7. Dan likes his macaroni on top of the cheese.
8. I saw Tom at open school night.
9. Carol won a diamond tiara, dishes, and a tape player.
10. Mom helped me with my math, so in return I peeled potatoes for dinner.

Illustrated by Paul Richer

Answer on page 49.

THE CASE OF THE FARAWAY FRIEND

Read the story and fill in the missing words. Then match the numbered letters with the corresponding spaces at the end of the story. If you've filled in the spaces correctly, you'll have solved this mystery.

Bobby Beagle, a little brown __ __ __ ,
                                      8
lived in a two-story __ __ __ __ __ in the
                      6
mountains. Each day he spent many happy

__ __ __ __ __ chasing the colorful
10

__ __ __ __ __ __ __ __ __ __ __ __ __ that
    1
fluttered among the flowers, barking at the

eagles, hawks and other __ __ __ __ __ that
                          11
soared in the blue __ __ __ above, and
                    12

teasing the hissing garter __ __ __ __ __ as it slid gracefully through the
                            15
grass. He chased leaves when the __ __ __ __ blew, watched the white
                                  14
__ __ __ __ __ __ __ drift across the sky, and enjoyed the red and gold
    7
__ __ __ __ __ __ __ when the sun went down. He was so busy and happy,
        3
he hardly had time to scratch __ __ __ __ __ .
                               9

However, Bobby wished he had a dog friend. One day, as he sat looking

down into the peaceful __ __ __ __ __ __ below, he opened his
                        16
__ __ __ __ __ __ and uttered a mournful "Woof." Imagine his surprise
        2
to hear an answering "__ __ __ __" from the mountain on the other
                       17
side of the valley. Bobby could see a small figure on the side of that

Illustrated by R. Michael Palan

__ __ __ __ __ __ __ __ . He barked again and received a reply. He had
   13   18

found a friend. Each morning he sat under the big oak __ __ __ __ and
                                                         4

called to his new friend, who answered him immediately. It was a beautiful

friendship!

Now, of course, Bobby wanted to know more about that other dog, so he

asked Charlie, the big black __ __ __ __ , for help.
                              19

"Sure, I'll check him out," cawed __ __ __ __ __ __ __ , and he flew off
                                    5

across the valley.

Soon he returned. "Sorry, Bobby," he said. "That figure you saw was

no dog. It was a __ __ __ __ stump."
                  20

"Then who's been answering me all this time?" asked Bobby.

Bobby was being answered by:

__ __ __   __ __ __ __   __ __   __ __ __   __ __ __   __ __ __ __ __ .
 1 2 3   4 5 6 7   8 9   10 11 12   13 14 15   16 17 18 19 20

FOUR LITTLE KITTENS

Sylvester, Tiki, Chester, and Pete
Are four kittens with very cold feet.
These four little kittens
Have all lost their mittens.
Use the clues in this batch
To get the cats and gloves to match.

Illustrated by Margeaux Lucas

Use the chart to keep track of your answers. Put an X in each box that can't be true
and a circle in the boxes that match. For example, clue 3 says the blue mittens were
found in the woods. Find the box where blue mittens and woods meet and put a
circle there. Since the blue mittens cannot have been anywhere else, put an X in
every other location box that is in the blue columns.

1. Neither the yellow mittens nor Sylvester's mittens were found hanging on
   the fence.
2. Tiki found her mittens (not the green ones) near the duck pond.
3. The blue mittens were found in the woods.
4. The four kittens are: Pete, the owner of the red mittens, the owner of the
   blue mittens, and the kitten who lost his mittens in the barn.

	Blue	Green	Red	Yellow	Barn	Fence	Pond	Woods
Chester								
Pete								
Sylvester								
Tiki								
Barn								
Fence								
Pond								
Woods								

Answer on page 50.

NUMBER, PLEASE

Look, over there! Something just stepped out of that phone booth. Is it a bird with a bag of quarters or a mild-mannered reporter just changing his clothes? Use your imagination to draw in whatever you think it is.

Illustrated by Richard Johnson

HIDDEN PICTURES

How many objects can you
find hidden in this picture?

Illustrated by Kit Wray

WHAT AM I?

1. I am an electromechanical instrument.

2. In the early 1900s, Swiss music box manufacturers specialized in making small portable versions of me.

3. The inventor Emile Berliner invented a version of me in 1887 that is more like today's version than earlier models.

4. In my early days, a version of me was developed in France in which my arm moved outward, instead of inward.

5. Thomas Edison built the first practical version of me, intending to use it as a dictating machine in offices.

6. My four main parts are the turntable, the tone arm, the amplifier, and the loudspeaker.

7. My turntable has turned at a variety of speeds. Until about 1948, my most common speed was 78 RPM's. Today, my turntable can be set to turn at either 45 RPM's or 33 1/3 RPM's.

8. In my early days, I was known as a gramophone.

   What Am I?

Answer on page 50.

THE WORM RETURNS

Uh-oh! Wally Worm needs to wiggle a way home without joining Wendy Woodpecker for dinner. Can you help Wally return safely to his hole?

FINISH

START

Illustrated by Charles Jordan

Answer on page 50.

DOG DAZE

This crossword puzzle has gone to the dogs.
Many clues are about our four-legged friends.
How much of this puzzle can you solve?

Across:

1. Dog's coat, like a rug
5. Scram, cat!
9. Pet _____, place to buy a dog
10. _____ bear, from the north
12. _____ and behold!
13. A defined area of land or stretch of time
15. Short for Mother
16. _____ Baba
18. Missing in Action (abbrev.)
19. Outdoor place for dogs to run or something to write with
20. What a dog becomes at the dinner table
22. Good place to walk dog or play ball
23. Capital of England: _____don
24. Low water or food dish
25. See _____ run!
27. _____ retriever
30. _____ much!
31. Ghostly word
32. Much _____ about nothing.
33. All right!
34. Wear away the land
36. _____ fetch!
37. Move in and out between cones when skating
39. Full, like a ship
41. Outdoor shelter
42. Makes mistakes

Down:

1. The dog _____ that bone!
2. What Santa says 3 times
3. Short for Arthur
4. _____ shepherd
5. Group that aids and protects animals
6. Camp bed
7. Abbreviation for American League
8. Not as wild
9. _____ of bacon
11. Place or level in the standings
14. Dogs hang out car windows to get _____
17. Where a husky might live
19. Black and white animal from China
21. Managed to have
22. Man's best friend, a dog
24. French _____
25. Store away, like on a ship
26. Jabs with a finger
27. Sticky mess
28. Trims grass by sidewalk
29. Lunch time
31. Pure_____, a pedigree dog
34. The night before Christmas
35. A measure of corn
38. Sigh of relief
40. Abbreviation for Doctor

Answer on page 50.

Illustrated by Gregg Valley

4 5

HALLOWEEN AND VINE

These pictures are out of order. Can you number them to
show what happened first, second, and so on?

Answer on page 50.

Illustrated by Barbara Gray

ANSWERS

COVER

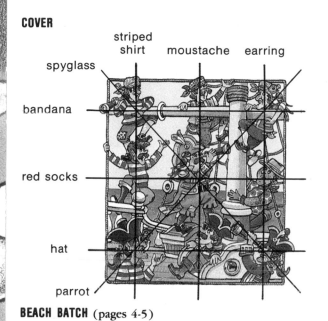

- spyglass
- striped shirt
- moustache
- earring
- bandana
- red socks
- hat
- parrot

BEACH BATCH (pages 4-5)

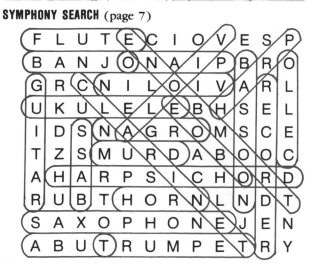

SYMPHONY SEARCH (page 7)

F L U T E C I O V E S P
B A N J O N A I P B R O
G R C N I L O I V A R L
U K U L E L E B H S E L
I D S N A G R O M S C E
T Z S M U R D A B O O C
A H A R P S I C H O R D
R U B T H O R N L N D T
S A X O P H O N E J E N
A B U T R U M P E T R Y

SPEAKING SPANISH (page 10)

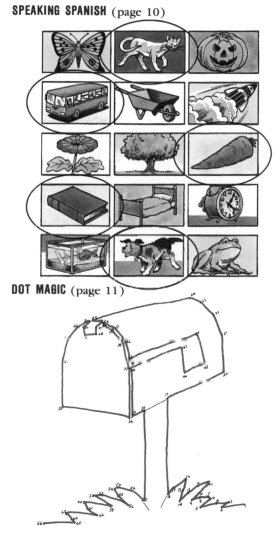

DOT MAGIC (page 11)

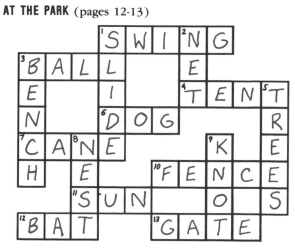

AT THE PARK (pages 12-13)

Across/Down crossword answers:

- 1. SWING
- 2. N
- 3. BALL / BENCH
- 4. TENT
- 5. TREES
- 6. DOG
- 7. CANE
- 8. E
- 9. K
- 10. FENCE
- 11. SUN
- 12. BAT
- 13. GATE

STAR SUMS (page 14)

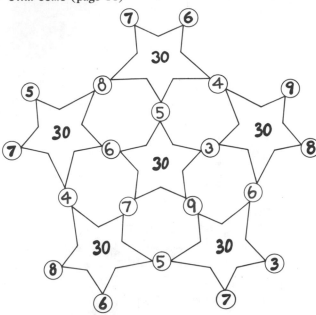

OFF-ROAD MEMORIES (page 16)

1. Chandler Woods Race Course (on sign)
2. Orange
3. 17
4. Blue
5. 2:00 p.m. (on sign)
6. One
7. Aldo
8. He had a flat tire.

ON THE SCENT (page 16)

By holding its nose

WHAT'S IN A WORD? (page 17)

Here are the words we found.
You may have found others.

able	bloom	mule
about	eat	oat
ail	elm	oil
aim	iota	out
ale	lab	tab
alm	lamb	table
alum	lame	tail
ate	late	tale
atom	limb	tame
auto	lob	tea
bail	loom	tie
bait	loot	tile
bale	mail	time
balm	male	toil
but	mate	tomb
beam	meal	tool
beat	metal	tuba
belt	mile	tube
blame	mite	U-boat
bleat	moat	ultima
bloat	mobile	

LOOK OUT BELOW! (pages 18-19)

S	Q	U	I	D	N	A	P	P	E	R	S
1	2	3	4	5	6	7	8	8	9	10	1

ONE WRONG WORD (page 20)

1. Women - Women did not vote for president during Lincoln's time.
2. Leaves - The ground in a pine forest would be covered with long narrow things usually called needles.
3. Passenger - There are no more passenger pigeons. They are extinct.
4. Days - It takes about 10 weeks to grow carrots ready to eat.
5. Glider - A glider plane would not need gas.
6. Quartz - A quartz clock uses batteries not electricity.
7. Astronaut - There were no famous astronauts in 1930.
8. Steel - Steel is not strong enough to cut a diamond. A diamond is shaped with other diamonds.
9. Contact - Contact lenses do not have frames.
10. Nonfiction - Nonfiction means something is real.

INSTANT PICTURE (page 21)

COMBO-CONNECTION (pages 22-23)

BRAID TEASER (page 24)

A FEW GOOD MEN (page 25)

1. amen
2. moment
3. mental
4. cement
5. mentor
6. menace
7. immense
8. abdomen
9. commence
10. pavement
11. filament
12. menagerie

PICTURE MIXER (pages 26-27)

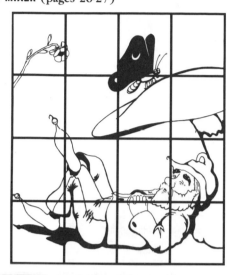

PARTY PROBLEMS (pages 28-29)

Please come to my birthday party this Wednesday after six o'clock. We will have cake, ice cream, and soda pop. We will dance, play games, and sing songs. It will be lots of fun. Hope you can come!

Love,
Penelope

Party supplies
1. candles
2. extra chairs
3. two packages of balloons
4. chocolate ice cream
5. some new games
6. prizes for game winners
7. juice for the punch
8. colorful streamers
9. borrow some records from Jim
10. red tablecloth
11. funny hats
12. noisemakers

SIZE WISE (page 30)

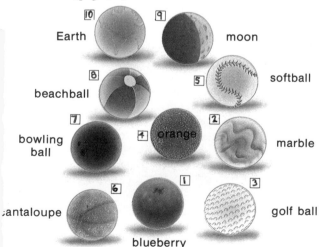

Earth — 10
moon — 9
beachball — 8
softball — 5
bowling ball — 7
orange — 4
marble — 2
cantaloupe — 6
blueberry — 1
golf ball — 3

STOP, LOOK, AND LIST (page 31)

These are the answers we found. You may have found some others.

Places to Meet People	Insects	Metals
Convention	Cockroach	Copper
Auditorium	Ant	Aluminum
Gallery	Grasshopper	Gold
Museum	Mosquito	Mercury
Theater	Tick	Tin

GEOLOGY GEMS (pages 32-33)

What musical group do geologists go to see at rock concerts? The Rolling Stones

What is a geologist's favorite candy? Rock Candy

RAINBOW ROUND-UP (page 34)

1. green
2. red
3. blue
4. black
5. orange
6. white
7. yellow
8. purple

VEGETABLE SOUP (page 35)

1. Bean, in the words: be an
2. Pea, in the words: recipe again
3. Okra, in the words: took rabbit
4. Beet, in the words: be Etruscan
5. Yam, in the words: why am
6. Kale, in the words: Rifka let
7. Onion, in the words: macaroni on
8. Tomato, in the words: Tom at open
9. Radish, in the words: tiara dishes
10. Turnip, in the words: return I peeled

THE CASE OF THE FARAWAY FRIEND (pages 36-37)

Bobby Beagle, a little brown DOG, lived in a two-story HOUSE in the mountains. Each day he spent many happy HOURS chasing the colorful BUTTERFLIES that fluttered among the flowers, barking at the eagles, hawks and other BIRDS that soared in the blue SKY above, and teasing the hissing garter SNAKE as it slid gracefully through the grass. He chased leaves when the WIND blew, watched the white CLOUDS drift across the sky, and enjoyed the red and gold SUNSET when the sun went down. He was so busy and happy, he hardly had time to scratch FLEAS.

However, Bobby wished he had a dog friend. One day, as he sat looking down into the peaceful VALLEY below, he open his MOUTH and uttered a mournful "Woof." Imagine his surprise to hear an answering "WOOF" from the mountain on the other side of the valley. Bobby could see a small figure on the side of that MOUNTAIN. He barked again and received a reply. He had found a friend. Each morning he sat under the big oak TREE and called to his new friend, who answered him immediately. It was a beautiful friendship!

Now, of course, Bobby wanted to know more about that other dog, so he asked Charlie, the big black CROW, for help.

"Sure, I'll check him out," cawed CHARLIE, and he flew off across the valley.

Soon he returned. "Sorry, Bobby," he said. "That figure you saw was no dog. It was a TREE stump."

"Then who's been answering me all this time?" asked Bobby.

Bobby was being answered by:

T H E   E C H O   O F   H I S   O W N   V O I C E
1 2 3   4 5 6 7   8 9   10 11 12   13 14 15   16 17 18 19 20

FOUR LITTLE KITTENS (page 38)

Tiki's mittens were found near the duck pond (clue 2). Pete's mittens were not blue or red (clue 4), so his mittens were not found in the woods (clue 3). Also, his mittens were not in the barn (clue 4), so Pete's mittens were on the fence. Since they can't be red or blue, and they can't be yellow (clue 1), Pete's mittens must be green.

The mittens lost in the barn are not blue or red (clue 4), and they can't be green (see above), so they must be yellow. Since the blue mittens were found in the woods (clue 3), the only place left for the red ones is near the pond. Since Tiki's mittens were found near the pond, the red ones belong to her.

Since Sylvester's mittens were not yellow (clue 1), nor were they red or green, they must be blue, and they were in the woods. By elimination, Chester is left with the yellow mittens, which were found in the barn.

	Blue	Green	Red	Yellow	Barn	Fence	Pond	Woods
Chester	X	X	X	O	O	X	X	X
Pete	X	O	X	X	X	O	X	X
Sylvester	O	X	X	X	X	X	X	O
Tiki	X	X	O	X	X	X	O	X
Barn	X	X	X	O				
Fence	X	O	X	X				
Pond	X	X	O	X				
Woods	O	X	X	X				

WHAT AM I? (page 42)

Phonograph (or record player)

THE WORM RETURNS (page 43)

DOG DAZE (pages 44-45)

S	H	A	G		S	C	A	T
S	T	O	R	E		P	O	L	A	R

(crossword grid)

S H A G — S C A T
S T O R E — P O L A R
L O — T R A C T — M A
A L I — M I A — P E N
B E G G A R — P A R K
L O N — P A N
S P O T — G O L D E N
T O O — B O O — A D O
O K — E R O D E — G O
W E A V E — L A D E N
S H E D — E R R S

HALLOWEEN AND VINE (page 46)

5	3
6	1
2	4

Editor: Jeffrey A. O'Hare • **Art Director:** Timothy J. Gillner
Project Director: Pamela Gallo • **Editorial Consultant:** Andrew Gutelle
Design Consultant: Bob Feldgus

Puzzle Contributors
Genevieve Bylinowski • James Dorr • Debbie Driscoll • Virginia Kroll • Marie Latta • Jan Onffroy • Donna Lugg Pape
Marilyn Senterfitt • Bette Sondike • Verda Spickelmier • Sherry Timberman • F. D. Uptain • Jackie Vaughan